Henry W Howgate

Proposed Legislation, Correspondence and Action

of scientific and commercial associations in reference to polar colonization

Henry W Howgate

Proposed Legislation, Correspondence and Action
of scientific and commercial associations in reference to polar colonization

ISBN/EAN: 9783337161996

Printed in Europe, USA, Canada, Australia, Japan

Cover: Foto ©Suzi / pixelio.de

More available books at **www.hansebooks.com**

Proposed Legislation,

Correspondence,

and Action of

Scientific and Commercial

Associations

in Reference to

Polar Colonization.

PROPOSED LEGISLATION.

A BILL to authorize and equip an expedition to the Arctic
Seas:

"*Be it enacted by the Senate and House of Representatives of
the United States of America in Congress assembled,* That the
President of the United States be authorized to organize
and send out one or more expeditions toward the North Pole,
and to establish a temporary colony, for purposes of exploration, at some point north of the eighty-first degree of north
latitude, on or near the shore of Lady Franklin Bay; to
detail such officers or other persons of the public service to
take part in the same as may be necessary, and to use any
public vessel that may be suitable for the purpose; the
scientific operations of the expedition to be prosecuted in
accordance with the advice of the National Academy of
Science; and that the sum of fifty thousand dollars, or such
part thereof as may be necessary, be hereby appropriated out
of any moneys in the Treasury not otherwise appropriated,
to be expended under the direction of the President: *Provided,* That no part of the sum so appropriated shall be carried to the surplus fund or covered into the Treasury until
the purposes of the appropriation shall have been com-
pleted, but may be applied to expenses of said expedition
incurred during any subsequent year that said expedition
may be engaged in its duties."

[Introduced in the House of Representatives, January 8, 1877, by Mr. Hunter, of Indiana. Read twice, referred to the Committee on Naval Affairs, and
ordered to printed.

Introduced in the Senate of the United States, February 9, 1877, by Mr.
Dawes, of Massachusetts. Read twice and referred to the Committee on Naval
Affairs.

Reported favorably from House Committee on Naval Affairs, February 22,
1877, by Mr. Willis, (Report No. 181,) and recommitted and ordered to be
printed.]

POLAR COLONIZATION.

The following selections are made from the numerous communications received favoring the Polar Colonization plan in its essential features, to show the general feeling of interest in the subject among explorers and men of science.

(From the President of the American Geographical Society.)
AMERICAN GEOGRAPHICAL SOCIETY,
No. 11 W. 29TH ST., NEW YORK CITY,
January 18th, 1877.

Captain H. W. Howgate:

MY DEAR SIR: Before your letter was received I inserted in my annual address a notice of your plan and of the bill before Congress.

As you will find by my address, your mode of exploration is the one that I have uniformly approved and recommended for many years. I expressed this opinion in my address of 1869, and in the first of my addresses, which have been printed, (1870,) I declared my conviction that a passage to the Pole by water would, in all probability, not be found, and that the true method of exploration was by sledge operations upon land from the furthest point that could be safely reached by a vessel.

* * * * * * * *

You will see from this that I have long been impressed with your general plan, and the only criticism I have to offer is that I think the station should not be limited to some point north of 81°; for though a vessel may winter securely in Discovery Bay, and although there is a fine seam of bituminous coal three miles from where the *Discovery* wintered, yet the region, as shown by the experience of the English expedition and by the abandonment of the Esquimaux settlements just below it, is very barren of animal life either upon the land or upon the water, whilst at Fort Foulke it is otherwise, and a temporary colony could be maintained there without any difficulty. For this reason I think it would have been better to have said north of 78°

It will afford me great pleasure to do all that I can to forward your views, and anything that the Society can do I am sure will be done.

The suggestion I have made as to the limitation in the bill as to location of colony is entirely for your consideration, and will in no way affect our hearty support of the measure.

*   *   *   *   *   *   *   *

Very truly yours,

CHAS. P. DALY.

(From Prof. Elias Loomis, of Yale College.)

YALE COLLEGE, *January* 14, 1877.

Capt. H. W. Howgate:

DEAR SIR: I have received your letter of January 7th, together with a copy of a bill to be presented to Congress, asking for an appropriation to defray the expense of another expedition towards the North Pole. I have for many years taken a deep interest in Polar expeditions, and see no reason for abandoning further effort because former expeditions have not accomplished all that was expected. If we review the entire history of Polar expeditions since Captain Parry's first voyage, more than half a century ago, we find that every expedition has proved in some sense a failure; that is, has accomplished less than was anticipated; and some may therefore conclude that all the labor which has been expended on this Polar problem has been wasted. I take a very different view of the subject, and consider that the results of the many Polar expeditions, from the first voyage of Captain Parry to the present time, are worth far more than all the money and labor which have been expended on them.

In order to estimate the value of the results of these expeditions we should consider what would have been the state of our knowledge of the physics of the globe if no such expeditions had been undertaken. There is scarcely a problem relating to the physics of the globe which can be fully understood without a knowledge of the phenomena within the Polar regions. Whatever phenomena we may wish to investigate, it is of special importance to determine its maximum and minimum values, and in nearly all questions of terrestrial physics one or other of these values is found in the neighborhood of the Pole. If, for example, we wish to determine the distribution of temperature upon the surface of the globe, it is specially important to determine the extremes of temperature, one of which is to be found near the equator and the other near the Poles. If we wish to investigate the system of circulation of the winds, our investigation would be sadly deficient without a knowledge of the phenomena in the Polar regions.

If we wish to study the fluctuations in the pressure of the atmosphere, whether periodical or accidental, we cannot be sure that we understand the phenomena in the middle latitudes unless we know what takes place in the Polar regions. If we wish to investigate the currents of the ocean, we find indications of currents coming from the Polar regions, and it is important to be able to trace these currents to their source. If we wish to investigate the laws of the tides, we need observations from every ocean; and observations in the Arctic regions have a special value on account of their distance from the place where the daily tidal wave takes its origin. If we wish to study the phenomena of atmospheric electricity and of auroral exhibitions, no part of the world is more important than the Polar regions. If we wish to study the phenomena of terrestrial magnetism, observations in the Polar regions have a special value, since it is here the dipping needle assumes a vertical position and the intensity of the earth's magnetism is the greatest. If we wish to determine the dimensions and figures of the earth, we require to know the length of a degree of latitude where it is greatest and also where it is least. If we wish to determine how the force of gravity varies in different parts of the world, we require observations of the second's pendulum both where it is greatest and where it is least. In short, there is no problem connected with the physics of the globe which does not demand observations from the Polar regions, and generally the Poles and the Equator are more important as stations of observation than any other portions of the earth's surface. If the information which has been acquired upon the various subjects in the numerous Polar expeditions of the last half century were annihilated, it would leave an immense chasm which would greatly impair the value of the researches which have been made in other parts of the world.

The subjects to which I have here referred are scientific rather than commercial; but many of them have an important bearing upon questions which affect the commerce of the globe. In the attempts which are now being made by the joint efforts of the principal nations of the globe to determine the laws of storms, if we could have daily observations from a group of stations within the Arctic circle, it is believed that they would prove of the highest value in enabling us to explain the phenomena of the middle latitudes. Every winter upon the eastern side of the Rocky Mountains we find an intensely cold wave moving down from the northward and spreading over a large portion of the United States. How can we fully understand the cause of the great changes of temperature which so frequently occur during the winter months unless we know where this cold air comes from? And how can this be determined without fixed stations of observation extending northward over the Polar regions?

The vast extension of the commerce of the world in recent times and its increased security are due in no small degree to more accurate information respecting the physics of the globe, including such subjects as the mean direction and force of the prevailing winds; the laws of storms; the use of the barometer in giving warning of approaching violent winds; the surest mode of escaping the violence of a storm when overtaken by a gale; the most advantageous route from one part to another; the direction and velocity of the current in every ocean; the variation of the magnetic needle in all latitudes, and its changes from year to year; together with many other problems; and most of these investigations have been greatly facilitated by observations which have been made within the Arctic regions. I do not regard it as any exaggeration to claim that the benefits which have resulted both directly and indirectly to the commerce of the world in consequence of Polar expeditions, are more than equal to all the money which has been expended on these enterprises.

Is any additional advantage to the commerce of the world to be anticipated from further explorations in the Polar regions? Undoubtedly. Precisely what these advantages may prove to be we cannot certainly pronounce beforehand; but upon most of the questions to which I have already alluded more minute information is needed. The demands of science are by no means satisfied, and we may confidently anticipate that any advance in our scientific knowledge respecting questions connected with the physics of the globe will impart increased security to commerce. If a steamer starting from New York and traveling northward could pass directly over the North Pole through Behring

Straits into the Pacific Ocean it would be a triumph of geographical science equal to the first discovery of America. Whether such a result will ever be witnessed we cannot safely predict; but past explorations have not shown that such an achievement is impossible. I hope we shall not rest contented while so much that is clearly feasible remains to be done and until the northern boundary of Greenland has been traced.

Hoping that your efforts to secure assistance in the further prosecution of this Polar problem may prove successful,

I am, with much respect, yours truly,

ELIAS LOOMIS.

(From Superintendent C. H. Haskins, of the Northwestern Telegraph Company.)

GENERAL SUPERINTENDENT'S OFFICE,
MILWAUKEE, WIS., *January* 24, 1877.

Captain H. W. Howgate:

DEAR SIR: Yours of 21st received. To work a naked wire through or on the snow it is only necessary to observe one or two points.

1st. The snow must be absolutely dry. This condition you would probably have in the Polar regions nearly all winter.

2d. Reduce the tension of your battery to the lowest possible point. To do this use a good conductor and instruments of as low resistance as practicable for the circuit and few cells of battery.

I really think that for your expedition, if you intend to establish stations 40 or 50, or even 100 miles apart, that a form of magneto machine, if made sufficiently light to be portable and with coarse helices, to give you a *quantity* current, would be the thing for you, thus ridding you of the nuisance of battery and battery material, freezing, &c. In this case you would use polarized relays, as more sensitive. Your great trouble will be, not escapes from grounds, but any good ground at all for your lines. In this case your only remedy would be a metallic circuit, which would require two wires, which would get together and bother you. With dry snow there is absolutely *no escape.* The insulation is as perfect as can be. I told you I had worked over one hundred miles with the line under the snow and on it.

Don't misunderstand me. I do not mean the entire wire
was covered, but it was blown down in places, sometimes
on the snow, again in it, and it worked uninterruptedly until the thaw grounded it. The fact of perfect insulation
may be tested at any time with the thermometer at zero.
Ground one end of a large battery, lead the other end
through a delicate galvanometer and then to snow on the
ground. You can't get any deflection, except such as results from *filling* the wire. There will be *no* escape.

The line from Marquette to Sault Ste. Marie, Lake Su-
perior, runs along the coast, over hills and through valleys
in the forest. During summer, when the leaves are out,
the line leaks badly from contact with the green leaves and
shoots. It is always leaky. In the winter it is blown
down, and, in spots, buried for weeks. It is in this condition in spots now. Yet I was at Marquette two weeks
ago, and not a sign of escape in the wire. It was perfectly
clear.

To produce the maximum effect your instruments in circuit should not exceed the resistance of the battery and line
wire. If you use an induction machine (a magneto) the resistance of the coils and line wire would be very light,
using No. 14 copper wire, and you could work long distances with 56 ohm relays polarized. I have worked two
50 ohm polarized relays with one of Kidder's magneto
machines, costing $8.00, used for domestic medical uses.

A magneto machine that a man could turn with a crank,
and not weighing over 40 pounds, with a commutator to
translate both currents in one direction, could be made
for you that would do your work. Or, you could use a
small Gramme machine, with a permanent magnet, as an
excitant.

The snow business is *all right*. Go ahead. If I can help
you, say so.

Yours, in haste,

CH. H. HASKINS.

U. S. NAVAL OBSERVATORY,
WASHINGTON, D. C., *January* 25, 1877.

MY DEAR CAPTAIN: You have asked me for my views
in regard to the best methods of conducting Arctic exploration. I take great pleasure in complying with your
request.

*   *   *   *   *   *   *

I am opposed to all spasmodic efforts to reach the Pole, because the chances of success are not commensurate with the necessary outlay. There have been comparatively few well organized Polar expeditions, and all these have endeavored to effect their object in a single season by a spurt, as it were. They have gone at erratic intervals, knowing comparatively nothing of the laws that govern the Arctic seasons; so that, so far as their knowledge of the meteorological and hydrographical conditions of the Polar regions was concerned, each of them stood an equal chance of success. Under these circumstances each expedition was justly regarded as an experiment. The failures that attended them were, in a great measure, due to a blind haste to gain their objects. That eminent scientists should have considered the quite meagre results as an ample reward for the expenditure of life and money, proves only the magnitude and extent of the scientific secrets which are locked up in the frozen North awaiting the intelligent and persistent explorer. The only legacies that can be considered of absolute value which these expeditions have left to the world are the feats of heroism and endurance that send the enthusiastic glow of admiration through the heart of humanity, the bloodless deeds of renown, and the immortal glory won not by triumphs over fellow men, but by victories over nature in its most forbidding guise.

* * * * * * * *

A ship bearing reinforcements and supplies should, if possible, visit the colony each year. No one should be compelled to remain longer than one winter either on the ship or at the station; and the commander should each year order home those whom experience has proved to be unserviceable or uncompanionable.

The band of explorers should spend each spring and autumn in making excursions in various directions and in paying minute attention to the accurate survey and delineation of the country traversed. Dogs should be used for draught. They are the natural teams of the country; they require little food and no clothing; they need no shelter; they are fleet and strong; they will serve as food to a famishing party and, moreover, they multiply so amazingly that, with proper precautions, the kennel need never be empty. The sleds should approximate in shape, size and material to those used by the Esquimaux. At least they should be fastened together by thongs of raw hide and should be shod with ivory. Es

quimaux should be employed as dog drivers to accompany
all sledge expeditions, both because they understand how to
take care of dogs, how to build, quickly and well, snow-
igloos (which are best suited for temporary shelter), and also
because they know how to hunt, which is a very important
consideration. Now, white men, with all their genius and
skill, while able to do these things tolerably after considerable practice, are totally unable while on a sledge journey to
make themselves as comfortable as the Esquimaux, who, at
the same time, need less food and clothing. Hence, the knowledge and aid of these hardy sons of the North should be in-
voked. A man with ordinary tact and judgment can secure
a willing service from these innocent and docile people.
*   *   *   *   *   *   *   *

A continuous effort would also afford an opportunity to
test men, and, in time, those qualified physically and men-
tally for the peculiar service would be secured. A long res-
idence at the station or on the ship—whether continuous or
broken by returns home for recuperation—would give an
experience in the modes of Arctic travel that would be valuable indeed, and that would insure final success. The service would be eminently desirable; and each year hosts of
volunteers would present themselves, from whom good men
could be chosen. Under proper management scurvy would
not appear, and if the quarters were comfortable and the
food plentiful and of the right kind, the men could live as
well and happily as in more southern latitudes.

In order to preserve the health of the crew, special attention should be paid to discipline. The men should not
be required to expose themselves so as to become very
cold or wet except under the most imperative necessity;
neither should any unnecessary service, nor service of ques-
tionable expediency, be forced from them. The great solicitude of a commander of an Arctic expedition should be to
keep up the spirits of his men, to banish all repinings and
disquietude, and to promote their happiness and thorough
content. Scurvy has no power over a man with a cheerful
frame of mind if only he has the opportunity to provide
suitably for the wants of his body. Exercise must be per-
formed cheerfully and with the mind interested, to be of any
service; enforced exercise rarely accomplishes the intended
results.
*   *   *   *   *   *   *   *

Land as a base of operations is essential for the best kind

of Polar effort, not only because thereby whatever advance may be made can be held, but because the value of the observations will be increased if made at a permanent station. Many routes present this advantage, and I would not presume to say, absolutely, which would offer the fewest obstacles to an advance to the Pole. I trust that in a few years every possible route will be faithfully tried.

But as an American and for an American expedition, I would unhesitatingly recommend the Smith's Sound route—the field in which Kane, Hayes and Hall won such renown—a field that still affords an opportunity to show the world what American pluck and enterprise can accomplish. It will be unnecessary to mention additional reasons for this preference. They will naturally present themselves to the Arctic student.

*   *   *   *   *   *   *   *

The United States has the right to consider the Smith's Sound route as peculiarly its own, and no effort should be spared to carry on in that direction the work of her illustrious heroes, living and dead. Her history contains no brighter pages than those that record their courage and endurance.

*   *   *   *   *   *   *   *

Your plan, so far as you have announced it, is so like mine that it seems almost unnecessary to say how heartily in symyathy I am with you in your efforts to organize a Polar expedition upon a sound basis. I trust that you will be very successful; that Congress will determine to carry on the good work, and that you will be spared to share its triumphs. Polar research offers more rewards in the way of national glory and renown than any other similar enterprise.

I am fully convinced that the flag of the United States can be planted upon the North Pole itself if the proper support be given to those who have the patience and determination to attempt and pursue the indicated plan.

When the Arctic regions shall have thus been made known and the necessary scientific observations secured, then the attention of explorers might be directed to the South Pole, and under a corresponding system that vast and unknown Antarctic region will yield up its secrets, and man will at last " have dominion over all the earth," and prove his obedience by attempting to "subdue it."

Very respectfully and sincerely yours,

R. W. D. BRYAN.

To Capt. H. W. HOWGATE, U. S. A., *Washington, D. C.*

(From Captain George E. Tyson, of the *Polaris*.)

WASHINGTON, D. C.

Captain H. W. Howgate:

DEAR SIR: I was very agreeably surprised to see your letter, published some time ago in the New York papers, containing a proposition to Congress to appropriate money, ship and the necessary equipment for another expedition to endeavor to reach the North Pole, and I heartily concur with you in the plan therein suggested as the most practicable yet devised. It is a matter of no little surprise to me that there has not been more of an outpouring of American enthusiasm toward the achievement of the success of this great enterprise, and that, too, when we consider the magnitude and great importance of the work. It is unquestionably a noble effort, and the scientific societies of the country would do well to unite in memorializing Congress relative thereto. Now is the time, and if this Government fails this year, through a spirit of parsimonious economy, to appropriate the means necessary to the furtherance of this project, England or Germany will, in all probability, secure the honor of this great achievement.

GEORGE E. TYSON.

(From Captain H. C. Chester, of the Polaris Expedition.)

To the Editor of the New York Times:

Having had some experience in Arctic exploration, and being familiar with its dangers and difficulties, my attention has been called to the letter of Captain Henry W. Howgate, published in the "Times" on the 26th of December. I beg to express my thorough approval of the plan submitted by Captain Howgate, as I believe it to be the only way by means of which the Pole can be reached. All future explorations tending to solve the mysteries of this extreme northern region will have to be prosecuted by means of gradual advances made from some main depot. Exactly the same idea was entertained by Captain Hall. When we were at the furthest point of land, about 82° 8″, in October, 1871, we looked at the so-called impenetrable sea of ice. Then it was moving ice and water. From its smoothness we felt very sure that when the colder weather set in we would have but little trouble traversing the channel in the spring.

We should have endeavored to have crossed Robeson's Straits, and would have tried to gain a point of land visible northwest of us, which land we called Cape Union, and which we calculated was some sixty miles distant. If Captain Howgate's suggestions of establishing a party at or about Robeson's Channel, or to the west of it, is ever carried out, I think these people would, by progressive stages, reach in time the much desired goal. As to the obstructions mentioned by Captain Nares, all I can state is that such impediments did not exist in my time. The reasons why I suppose they cannot be so formidable are founded in the following observations: When, in May and June of 1872, we lay with the boats and crew of the *Polaris*, twenty-five miles from the ship, on the floe ice, waiting for an opening in Robeson's Channel, in order to cross it, during four weeks' time the straits were blocked with ice, but this ice was all moving south. We found no opening for a month, and were unable to use our boats. This ice went southerly at the uniform rate of about one and a half miles an hour, and was never checked, save when the winds blew south or southwest. If, then, the strait was filled with ice moving southerly, such an impassable barrier of ice as Captain Nares speaks of must have been found at a point very much further north than the land designated by us as being Cape Union. I do not think there could have been much of an error as to the distance we supposed ourselves to be from this Cape Union, and the North Pole could not have been more than 420 miles north of it.

When Captain Hall and the writer undertook the fourteen-day sledge journey, when we worked our way along in the twilight, Captain Hall said to me, "I am satisfied that the only way to reach the Pole will be for us to carry our provisions across Robeson's Channel, to form a depot on the other side, and from thence take out parties. It is work we must lay out for ourselves this spring." I believe, had Captain Hall lived, he would have carried forward the work just as Captain Howgate proposes; that is, by establishing depots and making progressive stages. Captain Hall's untimely death, on the 8th of November, 1871, prevented his accomplishing this design. I think, in order to prosecute the plan proposed by Captain Howgate, there would be no difficulty in procuring thirty men accustomed to Arctic travel who would ultimately achieve success. As to fresh blood food, I am positive that, at least in the neighborhood o

Robeson's Channel, the musk ox can be found from May to October. I shot the first musk ox on the Polaris plane in 81° 40″ during the latter part of September. With the crew of the *Polaris* in the latitude of 82° we killed twenty-four musk oxen. I do not believe there would be any trouble in provisioning thirty men yearly with this fresh food. I therefore must freely indorse Captain Howgate's views, and say with him, "Let an expedition be organized to start in the spring of 1877, and I firmly believe that in 1880 the geography of the Polar circle would be definitely settled, and that without loss of life."

H. C. CHESTER.

PHILADELPHIA, *Saturday, December* 30, 1876.

(From Mr. Robert Seyboth, a member of Dr. Hayes' expedition.)

Capt. H. W. Howgate :

*　　*　　*　　*　　*　　*　　*　　*

I have not the slightest doubt if a sufficient number of energetic men, well selected and officered, can acclimate themselves to the terrible severity of Arctic winters, the greatest difficulty in the way of the discovery of the Pole will have been overcome, for such a party and depot could be used as a base of operation from which to push forward, in favorable junctures of temperature and their accompanying condition, successive posts, each one to be permanently held until the next was established, and until some favoring season made the open Polar Sea a navigable reality.

The great question to be answered in considering your scheme is the possibility of sustaining human life at such high latitudes for a sufficient length of time. I do not hesitate to answer this question in the affirmative. My own experience during a stay of nearly two years within the Arctic circle, and with an expedition that possessed none of the comforts and safeguards usually provided for Arctic explorers, warrant me to believe that a systematically conducted plan of colonization, such as you propose, would meet no insurmountable difficulties in the effort to sustain life and sufficient robustness to carry out the work of exploration. Scurvy, the great enemy of former explorers, can be entirely avoided by adopting the proper hygienic precautions, as has been fully proved by the late Captain Hall, who spent several years in succession in company of the Esquimaux, in perfect health and without assistance from the outside world.

It is a noteworthy fact that American whalers, who frequently remain two or more successive winters in the Arctic regions, do not suffer from scurvy while wintering, but are almost invariably afflicted with the fell disease during the homeward voyage. Why? Because they do not hesitate to eat plentifully of seal, walrus, bear and even whale meat, all of which is readily obtainable in the highest latitudes. To this diet I myself found no difficulty in becoming accustomed, and, consequently, did not suffer from scurvy until after the enforced resumption of "salt junk" or the homeward stretch. Granting, then, the possibility of colonization, I fully believe that the adoption of your scheme would strike at the root of former failures in Arctic explorations, for it substitutes the steady conquest, step by step in place of the spasmodic and unsustained efforts hitherto made at the sacrifice of untold treasure and the loss of great and noble lives.

Very respectfully, ROBERT SEYBOTH.

(Letter of the Secretary of the Navy.)

NAVY DEPARTMENT, WASHINGTON, *February* 2, 1877.

SIR: In connection with House bill No. 4,339, now in your hands, and which provides for another Arctic expedition I have to express a hearty interest therein and an earnest hope for the success of the plan. The successful sledge journey made by Captain Hall before his death, the concurrent testimony as to a Polar sea open in some seasons, and all the details of evidence from the *Polaris* crew, seem to show that success is possible. Qualified officers, I doubt not, will gladly volunteer for such duties as may be assigned the navy in connection with such an expedition. I am convinced, however, that no expedition should be sent to this dangerous and distant region except under the sanction of the strictest military discipline.

I have the honor to be, &c.,

GEO. M. ROBESON,
Secretary of the Navy.

HON. BENJAMIN A. WILLIS,
Of the Committee on Naval Affairs,
House of Representatives.

(Letter of President Joseph Henry, L. L. D.)
SMITHSONIAN INSTITUTION, WASHINGTON,
January 31, 1877.

SIR: Your letter of the 30th instant, asking my opinion
as to the plan of Captain Howgate for explorations in the
Arctic regions, and its utility in regard to scientific and commercial results, has been received, and I have the honor to
give you the following reply:

From my connection with the Smithsonian Institution
and the National Academy of Sciences, I am, of course, interested in every proposition which has for its object the extension of scientific knowledge, and, therefore, I am predis-
posed to advocate any rational plan for exploration and continued observations within the Arctic circle.

Much labor has been expended on this subject, especially
with a view to reach the Pole; yet many problems connected with physical geography and science in general remain unsolved.

1. With regard to a better determination of the figure of
the earth, pendulum experiments are required in the region
in question.

2. The magnetism of the earth requires for its better elu-
cidation a larger number and more continued observations
than have yet been made.

3. To complete our knowledge of the tides of the ocean,
a series of observations should be made for at least an entire
year.

4. For completing our knowledge of the winds of the
globe, the results of a larger series of observations than
those we now possess are necessary, and also additional observations on temperature.

5. The whole field of natural history could be enriched
by collections in the line of botany, mineralogy, geology,
&c., and facts of interest obtained with regard to the influence of extreme cold on animal and vegetable life.

All of the above mentioned branches of science are indirectly connected with the well being of man, and tend not
only to enlarge his sphere of mental pleasures, but to promote the application of science to the arts of life.

As to the special plan of Captain Howgate, that of establishing a colony of explorers and observers, to be continued
for several years, I think favorably.

The observations which have previously been made in the
Arctic regions have usually been of a fragmentary character,

and not sufficient in any one case to establish the changes of the observed phenomena during an entire year, whereas to obtain even an approximation to the general law of changes a number of years are required.

It may be proper to state, in behalf of the National Academy of Sciences, that should Congress make the necessary appropriation for this enterprise, the Academy will cheerfully give a series of directions as to the details of the investigations to be made, and the best methods to be employed.

I have the honor to be, very respectfully,
Your obedient servant,
JOSEPH HENRY,
Secretary Smithsonian Institution,
President National Academy of Sciences.

Hon. BENJ. A. WILLIS,
House of Representatives.

(Letter of Admiral David D. Porter.)

WASHINGTON, D. C., *January 31, 1877.*

SIR: I beg leave to acknowledge the receipt of your note of January 30, with accompanying pamphlet, in relation to Polar colonization and exploration.

I have examined the pamphlet with the care that the importance of the subject demands.

I have always been an advocate for Arctic exploration, in whatever form it might be undertaken, and I think there would be no greater difficulty in carrying out an enterprise in the manner you propose than there would be in a ship. In fact, if an expedition was properly fitted out in the first instance, and landed in good condition at the point proposed as headquarters, it would be less hampered if the ship should return home until wanted with supplies.

In my opinion, there is an open sea for two hundred miles toward the Pole; that there are high mountains, from which are precipitated the icebergs which lately blocked up Robeson's Channel, and that had Markham's farthest point been exceeded by sixty miles the pack would have been passed and open water reached again.

Every few years we must expect just such a pack as Captain Nares encountered, which will probably last for a year or two, and will then break up.

If, at the moment of breaking up, men and boats are in readiness to take advantage of the opportunity, a great advance could be made toward the Pole.

There are no greater hardships to be encountered as high as 83° than have heretofore been surmounted by the intrepid explorers of the Arctic regions, and when we reflect that a party from the *Polaris* drifted eighteen hundred miles on a cake of ice, and that an infant and its mother were all that time exposed to the inclemencies of the Arctic regions, we ought to have no doubts about a company of strong, active men, well provided with everything necessary to make life endurable in that desolate region.

Certainly no weather can be more severe than that encountered by the officers and men of the *Alert* and *Discovery*, who experienced a temperature of 100° below the freezing point. It would seem that there are actually no drawbacks in the way of weather which have not been encountered before, and we are able to make every preparation to meet the difficulties in our way.

It becomes now simply a question of hardy men with brave hearts and cheerful dispositions, provided with an ample stock of the best provisions, and with means of amusement to make the winter nights pass as speedily as possible. The greatest difficulty will be to keep up the spirits of the men, and this matter should be very seriously considered in selecting the individuals for an expedition of this kind. Nostalgia is the great enemy you would have to fear; and if every man should be obliged to understand some mechanical pursuit which he could follow when the party was laid up for the winter, it would go far toward bringing about a successful issue.

In the event of such an expedition as you propose, I see a fine opportunity of utilizing the electric telegraph. Wires could be laid along on the ground or ice without much danger of their being carried off by bears or foxes.

I am no believer in a northwest passage for any practical purposes, but I do believe that there are a number of scientific subjects that can be better demonstrated at the North Pole than anywhere else, and I think we owe it to ourselves to know all about a matter which has hitherto remained in comparative obscurity.

In establishing your colony I would particularly suggest that a number of houses be erected and somewhat separated. That of itself would tend to create a diversion by causing the men to visit each other frequently. It would be well, however, to have one central depot under the eye of the commanding officer, where the command could be assembled as occasion might require. These houses could be made in sections and put up at the end of the voyage. They should be lined with thick felt, and would be very comfortable.

In connection with the proposed expedition, I recommend a combination of sledge and boat, somewhat after the plan of the gutta-percha or kerite-rubber life-rafts used in the Navy. They could be made very light for carrying packs, and when forced to take the water could be navigated with safety. If such appliances had been more used in Arctic explorations many lives might have been saved.

In conclusion, permit me to say that I can see no objection whatever to your plan, and hope you may meet with the success your energy deserves.

Very respectfully, yours,

DAVID D. PORTER, *Admiral.*

Capt. H. W. HOWGATE, U. S. A.,
  Signal Office, Washington, D. C.

(Letter of Rear-Admiral Charles H. Davis.)

NAVAL OBSERVATORY,
WASHINGTON, D. C., *January 31, 1877.*

SIR: I have the honor to acknowledge the receipt of your communication of the 30th instant, and to say in reply, that the plan for Arctic exploration proposed by Captain Howgate, United States Signal Corps, meets my entire concurrence and approval.

The general principles laid down by Captain Howgate for the conduct of future Arctic expeditions seem to be universally adopted. These principles originated in the recent expedition under Captain Hall.

Very respectfully, your obedient servant,

C. H. DAVIS,
  Rear-Admiral, Superintendent

Hon. BENJ. A. WILLIS,
  Chairman Sub-committee on Naval Affairs,
  House of Representatives.

(Letter of Dr. Isaac I. Hayes, Arctic Explorer.)

STATE OF NEW YORK, ASSEMBLY CHAMBER,
ALBANY, *February* 12, 1877.

MY DEAR SIR: I am glad to see you are getting on so
well with your proposed expedition, and that the matter is
in such good hands. You can, of course, always rely upon
me for any assistance in my power. I think your scheme
feasible, and trust sincerely that you will obtain the necessary appropriation. Your general plan is a good one, and
how fully I am in accord with it you may judge from a
paper read by me before the Geographical Society in New
York, November 12, 1868, from which I extract the
following:

"My views in this respect are in no way changed, but
rather they are confirmed by events. I give this simple
enumeration of its advantages: 1st. Land as a base of operation; 2d. The opportunity to colonize a party of hunters
and natives, as a permanent support. A glance at the map
will show you how important is the first of these elements;
the second requires a further explanation. The colony was
indeed the key to the plan which I had proposed for 1862.
Had I been able to return that year, I would have started
with two vessels, one a small steamer, the other a sailing
vessel as a store ship. Pushing through the middle ice of
Baffin Bay, I would have steered for Port Foulke, my old
winter harbor, at the mouth of Smith Sound. Here I
would have secured the auxiliary vessel, and, remaining only
a sufficient length of time to see the natives gathered
together and the wheels of my little colony set in motion, I
would have sought the west coast of Smith Sound with the
steamer, and through the land-leads have worked my way
to the Polar water. Failing to accomplish this the first
season, I would have secured a harbor for the winter, and
pushed on the work as opportunity offered. Failing alto-
gether, (in the event of finding the ice too closely impacted
at the head of Smith Sound to admit of a passage,) I would
still have secured my object, for, with a provision depot now
within six hundred miles of the Pole, with the colony at my
back, and in the winter readily accessible, with dogs breed-
ing there, and with furs and provisions accumulating, I
would have overcome the obstacles which embarrassed me
in 1860 and 1861, and which had embarrassed Dr. Kane
before me. Once in this favorable situation I would have
brought up my available strength from the colony, and in

the early spring, put out depots of provisions along the line of Grinnel Land, and following them up by a boat mounted or runners, I would then have sought the open water and the Pole. Such was my plan seven years ago. It is my plan to-day. I believe it reasonable, and experience convinces me that it is practicable. I even believe that the chances are greatly in favor of the success of the first part of the scheme; that is to say, that the ice belt can be penetrated with the steamer, the open sea navigated, and Behring Strait and the Pacific Ocean reached."

If you care to follow up the subject so far as my views are concerned, you will find them fully expressed in the Journal of the Geographical Society for 1869, volume 2, part 2. I think it will be evident to you that the great feature of my plan was that the colony at Port Foulke would be always accessible from home every summer, with as much certainty as any port in the world. Besides, it is one of the most prolific centers of animal life in all that region. Reindeer are numerous in its vicinity, my party capturing upward of two hundred during our ten months' stay in our winter quarters. During the summer, the air was teeming with bird life, and the sea was alive with walrus and seal. Bears and foxes were also numerous. Your extensive reading upon the subject of Arctic exploration will have shown you that men will not long endure the Arctic climate. Even Sir Edward Parry, the greatest of all Arctic navigators, found himself obliged to return home after two winters mainly because of the disturbed *morale* of his men. The long continued darkness of the winter, the entire deprivation of society, and the universal cheerlessness have a singularly depressing influence upon the mind, and you will therefore at once perceive the value of establishing a station where annual intercourse can be had with home, whence the sick and weary can be sent away, and new recruits brought into the field.

With Port Foulke as a principal station, and other points subordinate to it established on the coast of Grinnell Land up to Lady Franklin Bay and beyond, I think success would be assured in the course of three or four years. In any case, a vast amount of scientific information would be obtained at little cost and little risk to life.

Wishing you every success in your praiseworthy endeavor, believe me, very truly, yours,

I. I. HAYES.

Capt. H. W. HOWGATE, *Washington, D. C.*

Letter from Rev. Eliphalet Nott Potter, D. D., President of Union College.)

UNION COLLEGE, SCHENECTADY, NEW YORK,
February 15, 1877.

MY DEAR MR. WILLIS: * * * I have not noticed whether the bill for Arctic exploration has yet been reported; if not, as I understand it to be in your hands, permit me to say, for myself and the faculty, that we regard the measure with great solicitude, and hope much from its becoming a law. In the naturally intense interest which you feel in the presidential national question, don't fail to remember and to press this measure of importance to science and the welfare of the world.

It will be a proud thing for the practical genius of America to carry out the only feasible approach to the solution of a question, costing only a useless outlay of life and treasure so long as the end is pursued by the old method.

In haste, and sincerely, yours,

E. N. POTTER.

(Letter of Dr. John Rae, Arctic Explorer.)

2 ADDISON GARDENS,
KENSINGTON, 23d *February*, 1877.

DEAR SIR: I beg to thank you for the pamphlet you have so kindly sent me through our Geographical Society, giving your plan of an Arctic expedition, or a series of them, via. Smith Sound, a specially American route, by which I think there is much yet to be done.

* * * * * * * *

Your plan I think an admirable one, and I do trust your Government will take it up in a liberal spirit, and that suitable men will volunteer for the rough but most attractive work.

Having heard of your plan before I received your pamphlet, I yesterday sent off by post a long list of suggestions (founded upon my own Arctic experience and life in the Hudson's Bay Territories,) to the President of the Geographical Society, New York, with a hope that one or two of them might be useful.

Wishing you every success, believe me faithfully yours,

JOHN RAE.

Captain HOWGATE.

ACTION OF SCIENTIFIC ASSOCIATIONS.

(Action of Maryland Academy of Science.)

The following resolutions were unanimously adopted by the Maryland Academy of Science on Monday, February 19, 1877.

Whereas, This Academy has for its object the encouragement of science, whether abstract or applied; and

Whereas, There is now pending before Congress a bill to authorize and equip an expedition to the Arctic seas; and

Whereas, This Academy has been informed of the means to be adopted by and of the results which are expected from the expedition;

Therefore be it Resolved, That we cordially approve of the plan proposed, believing, as we do, that it is the one best calculated to lead to successful results, not in abstract scientific knowledge alone, but also in such scientific knowledge as will be readily utilized for the benefit of commerce.

Resolved, That we earnestly and respectfully urge upon Congress the passage of the bill.

Resolved, That the Secretary be directed to forward a copy of these resolutions to our Senators and Representatives in Congress, and request the careful consideration of the bill.

(Action of Franklin Institute.)

HALL OF THE FRANKLIN INSTITUTE,
PHILADELPHIA, *February 26th*, 1877.

The following preamble and resolution was adopted at a meeting of the Franklin Institute, held February 21st, 1877:

Whereas, A bill is at present pending before Congress asking aid for carrying into execution the scheme of Capt. H. W. Howgate, of the Signal Service, for reaching and exploring the region about the North Pole on the plan of colonization:

Resolved, That the Franklin Institute approve of this plan, not only for its economy, but for its efficient practicability, and believe it to be the most feasible plan yet offered.

J. D. KNIGHT, *Secretary.*

On motion, the Secretary was directed to transmit a copy of the above preamble and resolution to Congress.

[Presented in Senate March 2, 1877, and referred to Committee on Military Affairs:]

(Action of the Cincinnati Society of Natural History.)

To the Senators and Members of the Forty-fourth Congress:

The Cincinnati Society of Natural History respectfully represents to the honorable Senators and Members of the Forty-fourth Congress the importance of further and more successful Arctic exploration. In all the various branches of science are found important problems which can be definitely settled in the Polar regions only. The geography of that region is undecided. Hydrography and meteorology, two branches of science in which the United States are already pre-eminent, and a more complete and thorough knowledge of which is imperatively demanded by the ever enlarging interests of science, and of commerce, can no where be definitely settled but in the Arctic Zone. The laws of gravity are still uncertain, and can be decided only in the vicinity of the North Pole. Mineralogy, geology and all the branches of natural history still largely depend upon a thorough exploration of the Polar regions.

This society, therefore, in the interest of science and for the honor of our country, respectfully recommends favorable legislation on the subject of Polar exploration, and convinced that colonization is the most practicable way of conducting an expedition of this nature, recommends the passage of the bill to authorize and equip an expedition to the Arctic seas, now in the hands of the Committee on Naval Affairs.

The above memorial was unanimously adopted at a full meeting of the Cincinnati Society of Natural History, held Tuesday evening, February 6, 1877.

J. F. JUDGE,
Recording Secretary.

[Presented in House of Representatives February 10, 1877, and referred to Committee on Naval Affairs.]

(Action of Fortnightly Club of Milwaukee.)

Whereas, A bill has been introduced into Congress appropriating funds to aid and maintain a scientific expedition in the northern Polar regions; and

Whereas, The plan which is proposed to carry into effect an such expedition, namely, that of establishing a temporary colony consisting of a few tried and experienced men who possess all the necessary requisites to insure success of such expedition, seems to us the one most feasible after due consideration of the history of former expeditions which have been dispatched by the Government of the United States; therefore, be it

Resolved, That we respectfully request the earnest attention and support by our Senators and Representatives in Congress of the plan of Captain H. W. Howgate, of the United States Signal Service, as one which is in our judgment worthy of a trial and support by the Government.

Resolved, That the Secretary of the Fortnightly Club be instructed to forward to our Senators and Representatives a copy of the foregoing preamble and resolutions.

The above preamble and resolutions were presented at a meeting of the Fortnightly Club, of Milwaukee, Wisconsin, January 20, 1877, and unanimously passed.

WILLIAM W. WIGHT,
Secretary Fortnightly Club.

ACTION OF COMMERCIAL ASSOCIATIONS.

(Action of the Milwaukee Chamber of Commerce.)

CHAMBER OF COMMERCE, MILWAUKEE, *January* 13, 1877.

Whereas, This Chamber is desirous of expressing its interests in and good will toward all measures calculated to forward and extend scientific explorations and experiments which may have even an indirect bearing upon such subject; therefore, be it

Resolved, That we cordially approve of the proposed appropriation of $50,000 by the General Government to aid in the establishment of a temporary colony, for the purpose of exploration and scientific research, at or near the eighty-first degree of north latitude, under the direction of the President of the United States and with the advice and counsel of the National Academy of Science, to carry into effect such detailed observations in the sciences of meteorology, botany, geology and climatology, together with the perfecting of the geography of unknown regions extending to the North Pole, as may increase the sum of human knowledge, redound to the credit of the United States and sustain the reputation and honor of our country already won through the labors of De Haven, Kane, Hayes, Hall and other eminent explorers in the northern Polar seas.

Resolved, That the Secretary be instructed to transmit to our Senators and Representatives in Congress a copy of the foregoing preamble and resolutions, and to respectfully request their careful consideration of the same.

The foregoing preamble and resolutions were introduced at a meeting of the Chamber of Commerce of Milwaukee, January 13, 1877, and unanimously adopted.

[SEAL.]   N. VANKIRK, *President,*
              W. J. LANGSON, *Secretary.*

[Presented in House of Representatives January 20, 1877, and referred to Committee on Appropriations.

Presented in Senate January 26, 1877, and referred to Committee on Appropriations.]

(Action of the Indianapolis Board of Trade.)

BOARD OF TRADE, INDIANAPOLIS, *January* 23, 1877.

Whereas, There is now pending before Congress a bill introduced by General Hunter, of Indiana, appropriating the sum of $50,000 to aid in the establishment of a temporary colony for the purpose of exploration and scientific research at some point near the eighty-first degree of north latitude, under the direction of the President of the United States, and to carry into effect such detailed observations in the sciences, together with the perfecting of the geography of unknown regions extending to the North Pole as may increase the sum of human knowledge and redound to the honor of our country; therefore, be it

Resolved, That this Board of Trade favors the passage of the bill, and that the Secretary transmit to our Senators and Representatives in Congress a copy of these proceedings.

(Action of Detroit Board of Trade.)

BOARD OF TRADE ROOMS,
DETROIT, MICH., *February* 2, 1877.

Whereas, This Board is desirous of expressing its interest in and good will toward all measures calculated to forward and extend scientific explorations and experiments which may have even an indirect bearing upon commerce and navigation; therefore, be it

Resolved, That we cordially approve of the proposed appropriation of $50,000 by the General Government to aid in the establishment of a temporary colony for the purpose of exploration and scientific research at or near the eighty-first degree of North latitude, under the direction of the President of the United States, and with the advice and consent of the National Academy of Science, to carry into effect such detailed observations in the science of meteorology, botany, geology and climatology, together with the perfecting of the geography of unknown regions extending to the North Pole, as may increase the sum of human knowledge, redound to the credit of the United States and sustain the reputation and honor of our country already won through the labors of De Haven, Kane, Hayes, Hall and other eminent explorers in the Northern Polar seas.

Resolved, That the Secretary be instructed to transmit to our Senators and Representatives in Congress a copy of the foregoing preamble and resolution, and to respectfully request their careful consideration of the same.

(Action of Cincinnati Chamber of Commerce.)

CINCINNATI, *February* 2, 1877.

To the Honorable Senate and House of Representatives of the United States in Congress assembled:

Whereas, The Cincinnati Chamber of Commerce, whose province relates specially to commerce and trade, is assured that the security and extension of the commerce of the world depends largely upon accurate information respecting the physics of the globe, and that most of such information already acquired has been facilitated by observations made within the Arctic regions, and that the benefits accruing, directly and indirectly, to the commerce of the world from Polar explorations are more than equal to the money expended in such explorations; therefore, be it

Resolved, That we, in the interest of science, as well as in behalf of commerce and trade, mutually and inseparably linked together, heartily approve and respectfully urge the passage of the bill providing for another and eminently practicable expedition toward the North Pole for the purpose of exploration and the establishment of a colony at some point north of the 81° of north latitude.

Resolved, That we heartily approve an appropriation of $50,000 by the General Government for this purpose.

Resolved, That a copy of the foregoing preamble and resolutions be transmitted to our Senators and Representatives in Congress.

B. EGGLESTON, *President,*
BRENT ARNOLD, *Secretary.*

[Presented in Senate February 6, 1877, and referred to Committee on Appropriations.

Presented in House of Representatives February 6, 1877, and referred to Committee on Naval Affairs.]

(Action of St. Louis Cotton Exchange.)

ST. LOUIS, *February* 5, 1877.

Whereas, There is now pending before Congress a bill introduced by General Hunter, of Indiana, appropriating the sum of $50,000 to aid in the establishment of a temporary colony for the purpose of exploration and scientific research at some point near the 81° of north latitude, under the direction of the President of the United States, and to carry into effect such detailed observations in the sciences as may increase the sum of human knowledge and redound to the honor of our country; therefore, be it

Resolved, That this Cotton Exchange favors the passage of the bill, and that the Secretary transmit to our Senators and Representatives in Congress a copy of these proceedings.

(Action of Baltimore Corn and Flour Exchange.)

To the Honorable Senators and House of Representatives of the United States in Congress assembled:

Whereas, It appears that an expedition to the Arctic regions is proposed upon a plan which seems to promise a fair hope of a successful issue, at a cost quite out of proportion to the value of the least probable result; and,

Whereas, It is desirable that no efforts should be spared to determine questions in connection with the physical condition of the earth in the interests of commerce, agriculture and science; therefore, be it

Resolved, That we, the undersigned members of the Baltimore Corn and Flour Exchange, heartily approve of the scheme initiated by Captain H. W. Howgate now pending before Congress, and respectfully suggest that the bill now pending be passed with the appropriation of $50,000 to defray the cost of the expedition.

THOS. W. LEVING & SONS,
BARKER & GWATHMEY,
SAML. TOWNSEND & SON,
E. D. BIGELOW & CO.,
And others.

[Presented in House of Representatives February 1, 1876, and referred to Committee on Naval Affairs.]

(Action of the Baltimore Merchants' Exchange.)

To the Honorable Senate and House of Representatives of the United States in Congress assembled:

Whereas, It appears that an expedition to the Arctic regions is proposed upon a plan which seems to promise a fair hope of a successful issue, at a cost quite out of proportion to the value of the least probable result;

And, whereas, It is desirable that no efforts should be spared to determine questions in connection with the physical condition of the earth in the interest of commerce, agriculture, and science: therefore,

Be it resolved, That we, the members of the Baltimore Merchants' Exchange, heartily approve of the scheme indicted by Captain H. W. Howgate, now before Congress, and respectfully suggest that the bill now pending be passed, with the appropriation of $50,000 to defray the cost of the expedition.

BALTIMORE, *February* 7, 1877.

JAS. CAREY COALE,
JAMES BRICKHEAD,
H. O. HAUGHTON,
And others.

[Presented in House of Representatives February 1, 1877, and referred to Committee on Naval Affairs.]

(Action of the New Haven Chamber of Commerce.)

NEW HAVEN, *February* 9, 1877.

Whereas, The New Haven Chamber of Commerce, in common with so many similar boards in the United States, feel-

ing a deep interest in the Polar explorations already made
by our own countrymen, as also by those of other nations,
believe that the plan of Captain Howgate for the locating of
a colony far northward in the Arctic regions is the most
feasible of any heretofore projected for the successful exploration of these regions and for the discovery of the North
Pole, so long the ambition of so many expeditions; therefore,

Resolved, That this Chamber heartily approve of Captain
Howgate's plan, and, therefore, of the proposed appropriation
of $50,000 by the General Government in aid of the expedition.

Resolved, That the President and Secretary be instructed
to transmit a copy of the foregoing preamble and resolution
to our Senators and Representatives in Congress.

[Presented in Senate February 13, 1877, and referred to Committee on
Commerce.]

(Action of New York Merchants.)

NEW YORK, *February* 17, 1877.

To the Honorable Senators and Representatives in
Congress assembled :

The undersigned, feeling a deep interest in the Polar
Explorations already made by our own countrymen, as
also by those of other nations, believe that the plan of Captain Howgate for the locating of a colony, far northward in
the Arctic regions, is the most feasible of any heretofore
projected for the successful explorations of these regions
and for the discovery of the North Pole, do approve of the
bill now pending before Congress appropriating $50,000
for the establishment of the colony, and respectfully urge
the passage of the bill.

John H. Boynton, Boyd & Hincken, James W. Elwell &
Co., Benj. F. Metcalf, John Zittlosen, James E. Ward & Co.,
Gerhard & Brewer, Benham & Boysen, John Norton, Jr., &
Son, John D. Jones, J. P. Paulison, Thomas Hale, Arthur
Leary, Ellwood Walter, Alfred Ogden, Ferdinand Stagg,
Daniel Drake Smith, A. A. Low & Bros., Charles H. Mar-
hall & Co., Grinnell, Minturn & Co., Nath. L. & Geo.
Griswold, Thomas Dunham's Nephew & Co., Snow & Bur-
gess, Thomas J. Owen & Son, Howland & Aspinwall, Law-
ence, Giles & Co., R. W. Cameron & Co., George Wilson,
C. H. Mallory & Co., Youngs, Smith & Co., Jonas Smith &

Co., Johnson & Higgins, John D. Fish & Co., J. H. Winchester & Co., Lunt Brothers, Salter & Livermore, Floyd & Newins, Geo. W. Rosevelt, J. F. Ames, Wm. B. Hilton, Wm. A. Freeborn & Co., Smith W. Anderson, Bucknam & Co., John C. Smith, Perry Chubb, E. Sanchez y Dolz, Geo. W. Brown, Stephen H. Mills, F. Wight & Co., Baxter & McVoy, Philip J. Kiernan, Wm. B. Smyth, Fred. C. Schmidt, Thomas Norton & Co., A. K. Hadley, Theodore G. Case, Wm. L. Snyder, D. A. Hulett, Miles Beach, Robert Lyon, Jr., Edward T. Bartlett, J. W. Huntley, Francis H. Smith, Potter & Robertson, George W. Dow, L. H. Rogers & Co., Theodore Weston, Alfred Wagstaff, Jr., Abram C. Wood, John D. Vermeule, Henry Hentz & Co., Robert Dillon, J. Yeoman, Calvocoressi & Rodocanachi, James F. Wenman & Co., E. K. Powers, James S. Dean, Andrew G. Myers, J. D. Blanchard, J. H. Cheever, J. F. Fiske, Burkhalter, Masten & Co., W. H. Stanford, H. A. Howe, Wm. R. Crowell, B. F. Walcott, Levi P. Morton, and many others.

[Presented in Senate February 23, 1877.]

(Action of the Philadelphia Board of Trade.)

To the Honorable the Senate and House of Representatives of the United States the following memorial respectfully sheweth:

That at a meeting of the Philadelphia Board of Trade, on February 19th, 1877, it was

Resolved, That the project for the establishment, under the authority of the President of the United States, of a temporary colony for the purposes of scientific exploration, at some point north of the eighty-first degree of north latitude, meets with the approval of the Board; and that the sum of $50,000 asked of Congress for the execution of this design will be well repaid by an increase of scientific knowledge that will materially promote the welfare of mankind and the honor of our country.

The Philadelphia Board of Trade respectfully solicits your favorable consideration of the above, and will ever pray, &c.

[Presented in Senate February 23, 1877, and referred to Committee on Naval Affairs.]

Presented in House of Representatives February 24, 1877, and referred to Committee on Foreign Affairs.]

(Action of Nashville Cotton Exchange.)

NASHVILLE COTTON EXCHANGE, *February* 23, 1877.

Whereas, There is now pending before Congress a bill appropriating the sum of $50,000 to aid in the establishment of a colony in the Arctic regions for the purpose of scientific research and exploration, and

Whereas, This Cotton Exchange, in common with similar organizations throughout the country, and feeling that commerce and trade march hand in hand with science, and that such exploration and research would increase the sum of human knowledge and redound to the nation's honor; therefore, be it

Resolved, That this Cotton Exchange favors the passage by Congress of this bill, and that the Secretary transmit to our Senators and Representatives in Congress a copy of these proceedings.

———

(Action of Cleveland Board of Trade.)

BOARD OF TRADE ROOM, CLEVELAND, OHIO,
February 23, 1877.

Whereas, There is now pending before Congress a bill introduced by Gen. Hunter, of Indiana, appropriating the sum of $50,000 to aid in the establishment of a temporary colony for the purpose of exploration and scientific research at some point near the 81st degree of north latitude under the direction of the President of the United States, and to carry into effect such detailed observations in the sciences, together with the perfecting of the geography of unknown regions extending to the North Pole, as may increase the sum of human knowledge and redound to the honor of our country; therefore, be it

Resolved, That the Cleveland Board of Trade cordially favors the proposition and appropriation, and urges the passage of the bill, and that the Secretary be directed to send a copy of these proceedings to our Senators and Representatives in Congress.

———

BOSTON, MASS., *February* 23, 1877.

To the Honorable Senators and Representatives in Congress assembled:

The undersigned, feeling a deep interest in the polar explorations already made by our own countrymen, as also by those of other nations, believe that the plan of Captain Howgate for the locating of a colony far northward in the Arctic regions is the most feasible of any heretofore projected for the successful explorations of these regions and for the discovery of the North Pole, do approve of the bill now pending before Congress appropriating $50,000 for the establishment of the colony, and respectfully urge the passage of the bill.

Alex. H. Rice, Gov. of Mass., Fred. O. Prince, Mayor o. Boston, Jas. A. Dupee, Fred. Amory, Thomas Lamb, J. W. Brooks, Daniel Doherty, Addison, Gage & Co., Thaxter & Sons, Benj. F. Tyler, W. W. Russell, Jacob Hittinger Jacob A. Seitz, Dr. C. C. Folsom, Dr. Samuel H. Durgin and many others.

(Action of Wilmington Merchants.)

WILMINGTON, *February* 26, 1877.

To the Honorable Senators and Representatives in Congress assembled:

The undersigned, feeling a deep interest in the Polar Expeditions already made by our own countrymen as also those of other nations, believe that the plan of Captain Howgate for the location of a colony far northward in the Arctic regions is the most feasible of any heretofore projected for the exploration of those regions and for the discovery of the North Pole, do approve of the bill now pending before Congress, appropriating $50,000 for the establishment of the colony, and respectfully urge the passage of the bill.

De Rosset & Co., Alex. Sprunt & Son, Harriss & Howell, R. E. Heide, Edw. Kidder & Sons, B. F. Mitchell & Son, Lemmerman & Coney, Cassidey & Ross, T. C. De Rosset, Adrian & Vollers, Wright & Stedman, T. B. Kingsbury, B. B. Moore, (Hist. Soc'y,) Jno. L. Boatwright, J. J. Conoley, C. H. Robinson, Vick & Mebane, E. Peschau & Westerman, Kerchner & Calder Bros., John S. Cantwell, Donald MacRae, H. B. Eilers, Hall & Pearson, C. W. Harriss, Ed. Journal, Sol. Bear & Bros., H. Nutt, Williams & Murchison, John Wilder Atkinson, H. Q. Johnson, I. B. Grainger, Jos. T. Jamer, J. K. Brown, James & Brown, A. Empie, C. D. Myers & Co., Wm. J. Bühman, P. Heinsberger, Geo. G. Barker & Co., G. D. Bernheim, Prest. Hist. and Scientific Society.

[Presented in House of Representatives February 27, 1877, and referred to Committee on Naval Affairs.]

NASHVILLE, TENN., February 27, 1877.

To the Honorable Senators and Representatives in Congress assembled:

The undersigned, feeling a deep interest in the Polar explorations already made by our own countrymen, as also by those of other nations, believe that the plan of Captain Howgate for the locating of a colony far northward in the Arctic regions is the most feasible of any heretofore projected for the successful explorations of these regions and for the discovery of the North Pole, do approve of the bill now pending before Congress appropriating $50,000 for the establishment of the colony, and respectfully urge the passage of the bill. James D. Porter, Governor of Tennessee; James M. Safford, J. D. Plunkett, M. D., J. B. Lindsley, M.D., E. D. Hicks, M. Burns, J. B. Nowlin, M. D., D. R. Johnson, John Lunsden, Jos. Fisher and many others.

[Presented in Senate March 14, 1877.]

(Action of Merchants' Exchange, Baltimore.)

The Merchants' Exchange of Baltimore City, fully alive to the advantages to be derived from the development of Captain Howgate's scheme, for a further attempt to discover or, if unsuccessful, to at least familiarize the world with the circumstances and surroundings of the North Pole, fully endorse his plans known as the "Colonization Scheme," and heartily approve the adoption of General Hunter's bill, appropriating the sum of $50,000 in aid of the expedition.

BALTIMORE, 17th April, 1877.

JAS. CAREY COALE, President,
H. O. HAUGHTON, Secretary.

(From the New York Herald, May 20, 1877.)

THE POLAR COLONY.

Another letter on Captain Howgate's plan, from the accomplished Arctic explorer, Julius Payer, will be found in our columns to-day. It is a thoughtful contribution to the comprehensive study of this scheme of discovery, which seems to grow in favor with the writers on the subject in proportion as it is considered, either in the light of arguments in its favor or those against it; for it bids fair to be conceded that there is no objection to it that does not equally apply to a nautical expedition compelled to winter in the Arctic regions, while there appear to be several points of great importance in which it has a decided advantage over such expeditions. Our readers will find many objections fairly stated in the communication to which we refer, and we do not believe that they are made unduly prominent. No enterprise of this nature is to be conducted, even to that degree of success of which it is rationally capable, by shutting our eyes to the obstacles. Indeed, the choice of means for accomplishing an end confessedly surrounded with the greatest difficulties is a choice only between different sets of obstacles, and it has to be duly weighed which of these, if any, is absolutely insuperable. It is evidently the opinion of Payer that the difficulties in this case are not of that nature. It may be said now of this as of many other projects first scouted as visionary, that the conscientious study of its possibilities has placed it in the category of attempts sure to be made at no remote period in the future.

FRANKFORT-ON-THE-MAIN, *April* 1, 1877.

To the Editor of the Herald:

The Congress of the United States had recently before it a bill, which was referred to the Naval Committee, providing an appropriation of $50,000 for the establishment of a Polar colony. This colony is to be situated about four hundred miles from the North Pole, and to accomplish in patient leisure what the English North Pole expedition failed to achieve. The author of the project is Captain H. W. Howgate, of the United States Signal Service. Captain Howgate's plan is to plant a number of tough, determined and experienced men somewhere in the vicinity of the Arctic Sea. The place in which the *Discovery* passed the last winter has been considered most suitable for this purpose. The colony is to consist of fifty men, to be engaged for three years. A house in Lady Franklin's Bay is to be their dwelling place; an advance depot is to be established at the place where the *Alert* wintered, and to be garrisoned with a few men in the summer, and both stations are to be connected by copper wire and the necessary portable batteries. A ship is to be sent out to plant the colony, and then return every year to bring it supplies.

This plan for reaching the Pole is not only new, but also better than those on which the various expeditions by the way of Smith Sound were based. My personal wishes and views as to the Polar question in general I have already laid down in a previous article. I did this in the presumption that the efforts to reach the Pole would still continue despite all the objections that have been raised against their utility. For this reason, and because it is better that something should be done than nothing, every one will hail with great interest this American project, not so much from a hope of thereby reaching the goal, but from the probability of making new and valuable discoveries in a direction in which the United States have already won distinction. The following are the principal objections against Captain Howgate's plan:

In the first place, it may reasonably be objected to the plan of establishing a Polar colony for three years that such a venture would really be only a three years' Polar expedition without a ship—a North Pole expedition which discards a ship from latitude 82° north because it is useless to have one. But the advantages expected could only be reaped by changing, or rather renewing, the colonists and provisions every three—or what would be still better—every two years. To expect that within three years a condition of the ice will be presented so favorable as to render it possible for a division of the colony to reach the Pole, seems far too sanguine a hope; but by multiplying the projected duration of the colony, there might be a chance of reaching this end, and it would be unnecessary to support the colony every year by sending a ship; in fact, only steamers, and these, only under exceptionably favorable conditions, could succeed in reaching the colony.

Both men and officers could calculate to remain two years in the colony, as disappointed hopes and impaired health would render their efforts for the third year entirely fruitless. The colonists would be in every respect castaways, and their position would be even worse than that of the men stationed on the summit of Pike's Peak, Mount Washington, or at Fort York. Not much aid could be expected from the coal beds found by the *Discovery*. We found some coal deposits on the second German North Pole expedition in Greenland, but very few lumps of coal could be obtained without blasting.

According to Captain Howgate, the colony should only contain such men as would be capable of making scientific observations. The officers should undoubtedly be able to carry out all scientific labors, but I should be disinclined to engage for the work men not possessing the qualities which I mention further below (in discussing the question of equipment,) while the attainment of the North Pole remains the principal object of the expedition. I will now speak of the equipment of the expedition.

A SEAMAN FOR COMMANDER.

Perfect harmony in the conduct or direction of the expedition is the very first necessity. In modern times the direction of Polar expeditions has been transferred to scholars like Kane, Hayes, Nordenskjöld, Torell, &c. This course is permissible when the main objects of an expedition of small duration are discoveries in the domain of natural history, but not when the *rôle* of the seaman is an important one. Hence, the American expedition should be placed under the command of a seaman.

SELECTION OF THE CREW.

Next to the commander, the selection of the crew requires the greatest solicitude. It should be selected a considerable time before the starting of the expedition, so as to give the incompetent members an opportunity of making place for those that are peculiarly fitted for the task. It is this process of selection, and not its nationality, which decides the value of the crew. It is true that excellent seamanship is not equally distributed among all nations, but it would, nevertheless, require only sufficient time and proper care to procure in almost any country a model crew. It is often assumed that ability to endure cold must be the crucial test of fitness. This is an error. A sense of duty, endurance and determination are the most essential qualities. Habit soon overcomes cold. It often makes heroes out of sybar-

tes by the stern necessity of its endurance. Complete devotion to the object and to the commander presupposes
qualities which cannot often be judged in advance, and cannot either be purchased or sufficiently rewarded. The
members of an expedition should only be volunteers, but
not as was the case in the Russian expeditions, when the
officers were "chosen" as volunteers, although they had de-
clined to participate.

INTELLIGENCE AN IMPORTANT ELEMENT.

A certain degree of intelligence in the crew is of high
importance. In many instances they must have certain
powers of observation and reflection, and even a certain
amount of knowledge, to meet danger and reach certain results. But men who pass in a sledge from old to new ice
without noticing it, who pay no attention for several hours
to a frozen foot, who do not know how to handle their gun,
who do not observe the formations of the country through
which they are journeying—such men display an indiffer-
ence which, be they even as brave as Achilles, may jeopard-
ize the whole expedition. How great the indolence of the
uneducated can be may be inferred from Franklin's retreat.
His Canadians purposely threw away or destroyed the most
indespensable objects, such as canoes, nets, &c., to save themselves the trouble of carrying them. It was impossible to
make them deal economically with the scant provisions.
They resisted the orders of their commander, distrusted his
directions as to places and routes, secretly wasted their ammunition, the one stole the other's food, and the only thing
in which there was unanimity was the defiance of regula-
tions made for the good of all. The American Polar colony would be in a position scarcely less exposed than that
of Franklin and his comrades during their retreat. Seamen
are better capable of maintaining discipline under such circumstances than members of any other profession, and,
therefore, the colony should mostly consist of them.

HOW TO MAINTAIN DISCIPLINE.

The intelligent crew, by reason of its greater indepen-
dence, is one more difficult to lead than the ignorant. Devotion and blind confidence are rare among intelligent men,
and to control them you must set them constantly a good
example and act upon them by kindness and imperturbable
calmness. The first law of a Polar expedition is obedience
the history of Polar expeditions narrates the revolts of the

crews commanded by Davis, Barentz, Weymouth, Hudson
Hall, T. Ross and many others,) and its foundation is mor-
ality. Punishments are either impracticable, or, at all events
unreliable and irritating means of obtaining order. Thei
use, more especially in a private expedition, will sooner effec
dissolution than discipline. Coercion and threats remair
without results. It was thus fruitless to secure the success
of an expedition by compelling the men who had just failec
and returned to again resume their errand, a course adoptec
in the last century after every baffled effort to reach the goa
from the Siberian Polar Sea, when many a distinguished dis-
coverer was, after his return, degraded to a sailor. The bes
way of inciting meritorious emulation is to promise grea
rewards to the most deserving after the return home, bu
this should be done without naming the prospective recipi-
ents of such honors during the pendency of the expedition
As to punitive deductions of pay, the men seldom pay any
attention to such threats, and, with reason, because they
are seldom enforced upon the return home.

PECUNIARY INCENTIVES NEEDED.

For the officers the scientific achievements will be sufficient recompense for their labors, but for the crew only material advantages can constitute their satisfactory reward.
To be sure, money is but a weak incentive to men who are
destined to remain for years among the icy deserts of the
North, but it is, after all, the only means by which those in-
different to ideal objects can be interested in their attainment. The crew commanded by Captain T. Ross received
for four years of martyrdom, spent on the ice, only £100 each
The sailors of the second German expedition received from
eight to twelve thallars per month, but the crew of the *Tegethoff* were much better paid, and some of the sledge travel-
lers received as much as 3,000 florins ($1,500.) A power-
ful motor for herculean efforts may be obtained by grading
the amount of pay according to the success attained. Ir
1874 I guaranteed to the men who accompanied me in sledges
and should reach eighty-one degrees, $500, to those pene-
trating to eighty-two degrees, $1,250, and to those reaching
the eighty-third, $2,500, but in distributing these amounts
among them merit was to be a decisive factor. Prudence, as
well as justice, requires that the most deserving men should
be protected from want after their return for the remainder
of their lives. The crew of the *Tegethoff* all received perma-

nent situations through the State; the crews of the *Alert* and *Discovery* got high premiums, and all the officers were promoted.

I have dwelt somewhat extendedly upon the question of rewards, because individual experience teaches me their importance and because I presume that the new American expedition will call forth the highest efforts and the most genuine devotion on the part of its members.

WORTHLESS VOLUNTEERS.

Volunteers without special fitness or knowledge available during a Polar expedition—*i. e.*, volunteers who can offer nothing but their so-called enthusiasm, are worthless, and, if they belong to the better classes, they are finally found to be merely in the way.

Contrary to the general opinion, I would not recommend the employment of men who have already taken part in expeditions, except, perhaps, the most deserving among those specially fitted for the work. Others are but too liable to deem their own experience as valuable as those of the commander, and if their views conflict, to oppose a passive resistance, which destroys the first element of successful obedience. On the other hand, men who enter upon their first expedition are apt to receive the directions of an experienced leader with an attention which is generally only paid to revelations. Married men are to be excluded—a course adopted by Barentz (1596) upon his second expedition, while the *Tegethoff* had five on board.

The crew should consist of practiced pedestrians, mountain climbers and workmen. They should all belong to one nationality and be strong and healthy. The slightest indications of a tendency to rheumatism or affection of the eye and ear or certain other chronic ailments to which sailors fall but too readily a prey render them unable to bear the hardships of a Polar climate, and more especially of a sledge journey. They are like drunkards in this, that they are exceedingly liable to scurvy. Men under thirty are preferable to those above that age.

A PHYSICIAN, PHOTOGRAPHER AND PAINTER NEEDED.

The physician of an expedition should possess, besides his technical capacity, the most unconquerable patience, for to many of the sick he is as much a physician of the mind as of the body. Even if another doctor has already passed upon the physical fitness of the man, he should still subject them to a rigorous examination, for he alone is finally held responsible for diseases which may subsequently break out.

As an expedition should not only aim at its scientific object, but also at the dissemination of a correct idea or the aspects of Polar nature, it is urgently to be recommended that a photographer, and, still better, a painter also, accompany the expedition. A photographer is unfortunately circumscribed in the limits of his usefulness by the immediate surroundings of his ship. A good painter, however, could give us from the interior of the colony house invaluable studies of nature, and particularly of Polar light effects. They would be invaluable because none exist. On exceptionally fine summer days such studies could even be made in the open air, provided that oil and not water colors were used.

THOROUGH EQUIPMENT PREREQUISITE.

In the equipment of the colony in general the principle of providing the temporarily banished with the utmost possible comfort should prevail, as in all other Polar expeditions, even if subsequent experiences should baffle the efforts made in that direction. Ever since reading Kane's work, which I received as a school boy's prize, I have cherished the greatest admiration for that heroic man, as well as for Hayes, whose incomparable sledge journey has been always present to my mind as a lofty ideal. Experience, however, has taught me to warn other expeditions from starting with such insufficient preparations, and this note of warning applies especially to America, where enthusiasm and love of sacrifice go hand in hand. An expedition which lacks the most essential modern aid, that of steam power, and which (like that of Kane) has only scant provisions during the first winter and has to live on dried apples the second, takes place under conditions even worse than the winter sojourns of Barentz and Hudson. The smallness of the ships in the instances above referred to was partly the cause of the insufficient equipment. Small ships facilitate the passage through the ice, but, deducting the space required for the accommodation of those on board, for the machines and coal, such ships cannot hold supplies and provisions for more than two years and a half. The American colony, however, is to be equipped for three years; a portable house is to be erected, and twice the usual number of ship's crew is to be taken out. The only alternative, therefore, would be to select a ship of about the size of the *Discovery*.

HOW TO FIT UP THE COLONY'S HOUSE.

Among all circumstances, it is preferable that the members of the expeditions shall remain on board the ship instead of staying in such a house. The ship is warmer and there is less accumulation of ice around it. But as a house is to be erected and used, it should be fitted up for the special use of such an expedition in order to overcome the disadvantages I have named. Of course, the house should be made as dense as a ship, and the living rooms should be provided with watertight tapestry (vulcanized India rubber carpets and hangings.) The house should also be protected outside by a layer of snow several inches thick, and the windows should be covered up. To heat the rooms with ordinary stoves is not advisable, owing to their unequal distribution of heat, and this can only be secured by the feeding stoves, (Fullofen,) which possess the additional advantage of consuming less coal. The stovepipes should not lead straight up, so that the heat does not escape too, soon, but they should be distributed through the room. Hot air, conducted through pipes, is still more preferable, because it counteracts the formation of ice. Bricks will be found useful in some parts of the building. A separate chamber can be covered over with tin, and then used for washing, drying and bathing. The use of a bath in these northern regions is highly advantageous to health, because the skin receives no other friction. Petroleum will light the living rooms sufficiently, but in the cabins stearine candles are preferable to petroleum or train oil. Of great importance is the construction of lamps, (*i.e.*, observation lamps,) which should be used in the winter in the open air, and are not so likely to be extinguished by the blasts of the wind or to be frozen up. Even petroleum freezes at 20 degrees R. Massive grated circular glass lamps, of self-warming capacity, are best fitted for personal use in the open air. They are so popular that it is good to have quite a number. All doors should have latch-hooks and pull-weights.

SOME USEFUL HINTS IN MINOR MATTERS.

An important question in passing a winter in the Arctic regions is to maintain pure air and an equable heat. The first named requisite is secured by boring a few holes underneath (at the door) for the ingress, and above (at the ceiling) for the exit of the air, and covering them over with condensing vessels. The colony should also not omit to partially surround the house with outbuildings of stone or snow, which can be used for storehouses or windless passages and ante-courts, and these latter could be roofed over with strong canvas.

Discipline requires that the officers and crew should live separately. To transfer the kitchen, also, to the crew's room, with a hope of saving coal thereby, is not advisable, because it would too greatly increase the accumulation of moisture. As long as the men remain in the house they will not require furs, even in the greatest cold Close fitting woolen underwear and stout clothing will suffice in most cases, although the temperature in the interior of a house is lower than it is on shipboard. To take fur-lined leather boots is not advisable. They are of great weight, become stiff and soon lose their utility by freezing and by the wearing out of the fur. Boots made of seal or reindeer skin are preferable, but the latter should not be exposed to wet and ought to be covered with a cloth.

HOW TO SUPPLY THE COLONY.

The colony will have to suffer more from wet than even expeditions do on shipboard. The changing temperature and condensation of the water steam will exert a disturbing influence upon the instruments. Thick ice films will settle upon them as soon as the observer brings them into the living rooms from the open air, and then they should not be touched, but allowed to evaporate their steam. All instruments taken along by the colony should be cleaned by an optician without oil, so that they shall not freeze, and the gunmaker should do the same with the guns, whose barrels should be dark colored, so that they be less liable to rust. Ammunition, powder fuses for blasting the ice, as well as alcohol and petroleum, require tight vessels, and the last named two liquors should only be accessible through pumps that can be kept well closed. As for the rest, the largest supply of saws, ice augurs, shovels, ice creepers, handles, poles, leather boots, leather, water-tight linen, strong cloth, buffalo hides, flannel, &c., should be taken out. As to solid food, two pounds per man will be enough for the colony, but on sledge journeys two pounds and three-quarters will be required. This allowance should in-

clude one pound of bread and one pound of preserved meat.
Besides the usual other supplies, (in which salt meat should
be avoided as much as possible,) great quantities of preserved vegetable, cocoa, meat extract, rice, pea sausage and
dried farinaceous food (maccaroni, nudels, &c.,) are highly
advisable. Fresh bread twice a week, instead of the hard
biscuit, is very conducive to health. Indispensable are
plenty of tea and tobacco, and the latter, more especially,
is sadly missed by seamen. Instances have occurred
when the crew would smoke boiled and redried tea, lunt,
agaric, moss, and even paper, as they did on the Austrian
expedition. Moderate use of spirituous drinks is to be
recommended; their influence on health and good fellow-
ship is great. It is very difficult, however, to keep any
sufficient quantity of wine, more especially in winter, as all
sorts of wine freeze at five to eight degrees R. Even on
shipboard the preservation of wine is very difficult, and it
will be still more so in the home of the colony. It will be
better, therefore, to take but little wine, but all the more
good strong rum. The wine (often the best medicine for
the sick in these regions) and other indispensable liquids
can only be kept in the heated rooms under the tables, near
the stoves, or under the berths. To prepare chemical wine
during the expedition could be but a dreary makeshift.
Even the beer which the English expedition brewed on
shipboard from malt and hops would be found better. In
the colony's home the brewing will require exceedingly
light development of steam, and during extreme cold it
will be found impossible to produce fermentation.

A CHAPTER ON HEALTH.

The most careful solicitude should be bestowed upon the
election of preventives of scorbutic diseases. A ration of
lime juice should be issued daily, and all anti-scorbutic kinds
of food should be provided in abundant quantities. In itself
the Arctic air is not unhealthy; on the contrary, catarrh of
every description grows less and less, and even the exposures
to cold, such as are caused by the frigid temperature and the
sudden changes of the temperature, pass by without danger.
Whether this favorable condition is owing to a change in
the ozone contents of the air, remains to be seen. But, even
without the climate, there will be many disturbing influences,
many privations, labors, moisture; perhaps, also, the depressing effect of disappointments, and sometimes even insuffi-

cient opportunity for physical exercise. Polar expeditions
are not so dangerous or so frequently fatal as those in the
tropics, but infinitely more arduous. The vital powers,
however, are lessened year by year by the obstructions to
the formation of blood through the unfavorable conditions of
life, by the more or less unwholesome, because water-tight,
clothes, which repress perspiration, by the lack of fresh animal and vegetable food, the want of light and warmth, &c.
This diminution of the vital forces will require the renewal
of the crew in not more than three years.

HOW TO COMBAT SCURVY.

In spite of all care, however, in equipping the expedition—and a small library should be included for mental
occupation—I do not doubt that it will be afflicted with
scurvy. Apart from sufferings produced by severe cold,
the Polar traveler is not exposed to any form of disease as
much as he is to scurvy, and its appearance has the most
dismal effect. When it spreads to any extent the usefulness of the expedition is ended. Parry took the moisture
in the bedding as the principal cause of scurvy, and while
on Melville Island he used sorrel against it with great advantage. He considered beer as the greatest anti-scorbutic
of all drinks. During T. Ross' second expedition it be-
came manifest that vegetable food, more especially flour,
was of no avail in battling against scurvy. The consumption of fish, seal and train oil will, however, be found of
some benefit. Probably without reason it has been assumed that chewing tobacco has an anti-scorbutic tendency
in seamen, while the insufficient supply of water, the ex-
cessive consumption of salt or pickled meat, the uncleanli-
ness, the long and severe cold and the sensitiveness to it
have been deemed favorable to its development. Except-
ing the tropics, the experience has been that scurvy appears
most generally in the winter and spring, and it is, doubt-
less, encouraged by poor living. Nevertheless, even abundant animal and vegetable food form no perfect preventive
of scurvy.

In the absence of fresh vegetable food and of seals the
colony will be compelled to hunt land animals. Lime juice,
raw potatoes, sour fruit, (not mineral acid,) fresh vegetables,
wine, beer lees, exercise in the open air and cheerfulness,
important as they all are in preventing scurvy, do not, after
all, take the place of fresh meat in the Arctic regions.

even remember cases of men who neglected all these precautions, and yet, by eating plenty of fresh meat, saved
themselves from scurvy. As to lime juice, it is an excellent
preventive, but when the disease has once broken out, is of
little curative value. Temperature is of great importance.
During wet and chilly weather the patient will grow worse,
but in dry weather he will improve. In scorbutic affections
of the mouth it is advisable to take off the excrescences with
scissors and to pencil them over with muriatic acid. As an
additional preventive of scurvy I should recommend that
the crew sleep in swinging hammocks instead of berths,
thus escaping the danger of moist bedding. The patients
on board the *Tegethoff* recovered at once as soon as they
were transferred to a dry cabin, while the occupants of
damp cabins suffered more or less from scurvy all the time.

ABOUT SLEDGES AND THEIR CONSTRUCTION.

As it is the task of the colony to reach the Pole by means
of boats and sledges, I will give herewith my experiences in
regard to their use.

To accomplish the journey to the Pole with sledges alone
would require a coast along whose solid ice they could pro-
ceed, and which would terminate in a meridional direction.
As there is no mainland north of Grant Land, the boat and
not the sledge must be the leading factor of the American
enterprise. The sledges can only serve to bring boats and
provisions over the obstructive ice barriers. The success of
the expedition, however, depends entirely on the frequency
with which such passages must be effected, and with which
the boats can be sailed or rowed.

As to the construction of the sledges I would suggest the
following : The runners should be eleven feet long, two and
three-quarter inches wide, one and a half feet high and capable of supporting at least 2,000 pounds. They should be
made of ash, shod with steel and terminated at both ends in
soft curves. The ends should be high so as to be visible above
deep snow. At the back there is a contrivance for steering and
pushing the sledge, and this cannot be constructed too solidly.
The cooking machine should be made of one piece, and no
soldering is permissible, as it should be capable of developing
the intensest heat and prevent its escape, and, of course, as
little alchohol as possible should be burned. For holding
the alchohol little kegs of twenty quarts will be best. As
the journey to the Pole can only be undertaken in the sum-

mer, no tents or sleeping sack (schlaisack) is necessary, but it will be sufficient to cover the boats at night in tent fashion. Double-barrelled Lefancheur guns for bullets and small shot and copper cartridges should form the armament. Biscuit should be transported in bags, the other supplies in tin boxes.

ABOUT BOATS AND THEIR EQUIPMENT.

The boats should be made neither of tin, metal nor leather, India rubber or water-tight linen, but of wood. They should be large enough to contain the whole crew, with the sledges placed across them. The boats used by the Norwegians in the Arctic Sea ("Fangboote") are well available, except that their hold is too small. They accommodate seven or eight men, but on account of their sharp keel they can only be drawn with difficulty over the deep snow without sledges. It is, however, impracticable to draw boats for any considerable distances over the ice without sledges. To use runners for the transportation of the boats is not advisable, because they are soon worn out. The boats should be about 20 feet long, 5½ feet wide and 2½ feet high. The mast yard should be made of bamboo cane. Seven men would, according to the experience of the *Tegethoff* expedition, require the following supplies, apart from the results of probable hunting, for three months : Pemican, 245 pounds ; pea sausage, 400 pounds ; boiled beef, 400 pounds ; flour, 100 pounds ; bread, 250 pounds ; chocolate, 90 pounds ; salt, 15 pounds ; meat entrail, 10 pounds ; tea,. 4 pounds. To this should be added 240 pounds of alcohol, giving a total, without the boats and their inventory, of 1,800 pounds. The personal equipment of the travelers should consist of two woolen shirts, one wollen pair of drawers, three pairs of woolen stockings, leather water boots and caps, and a light fur coat to sleep in.

DOGS AND MEN.

Newfoundland dogs of extraordinary strength would be very useful in passing over the ice cakes, but in the boats they would be in the way. Although Esquimaux would be quite available in the colony, their appetite on the way north is enough to forbid their employment. As the expedition to the North Pole has only a chance of success if the sledges are used as little as possible and the boats find nearly constant free passage, it is self-evident that their crews should consist almost entirely of seamen of unusual physical strength.

As to the number of the boats, at least two or three should start on the journey to the Pole. From fourteen to twenty-one men are capable of separating with poles the obstructing ice barriers, (thus saving time in the passage,) to lift heavy boats and place them upon the sledges, &c. A smaller number would be nearly helpless in the face of the innumerable difficulties that are sure to present themselves.

In conclusion, a few remarks as to the chances of reaching the Pole from Grant Land. To accomplish in one summer 800 or 900 miles in an air line to the Pole and back in the Arctic Sea in boats—sledges being only useful in passing over obstructions—the expedition must find a pretty uninterrupted series of open water channels. If they find land they can easily penetrate along the coast to its highest northern point while the wind is favorable. Where there is no land the advance will depend upon the most favorable conditions of the ice, unless the expedition should be unfortunate enough to share the experience of the *Austrian* on its retreat, which accomplished only two German miles in two months. The most favorable moment for beginning the journey could easily be signalized by an advance post in the winter quarters of the *Alert*, but it will not be so easy to seize it, because by the time the expedition had reached the northeasterly corner of Grant Land it may have already passed by. The ice being still dense and intact in June, and still reaching far south, it is useless to attempt to force a passage where the breaking up of the pack into the floating ice some four or six weeks later secures at least a partially open water channel. Hence, the start should not be made before July, and even under the most auspicious circumstances no open passage of any extent will be met in Lincoln Sea before the end of that month. August affords really the best time for the journey, and at its end the retreat should begin, otherwise the expedition may become a prey of the new ice. For ships these channels will be impassable, but boats may force themselves through. The boats, again, lack the force of pressure and afford a smaller visual ken for a selection of the route. The only alternate is to pursue that direction in which the water reflection of the sky points. As to the distance which the expedition will accomplish per day, it may not be over a few hundred paces under unfavorable circumstances—*i. e.*, with frequent passages over the ice cakes—

but under more favorable conditions and tolerably open channels it may reach from twenty to thirty nautical miles. In every respect the passage through Lincoln Sea will closely resemble the retreat of the Austro-Hungarian expedition from Francis Joseph's Land. It is to be ardently hoped that it may be attended with equal good fortune.

JULIUS PAYER.